Unit 1

Simple present: *Wh* questions and answers

Question				Answer	
What	**does**	your sister	**do**?	She**'s** a vet.	*she's = she is* *he's = he is* *they're = they are*
		his uncle		He**'s** a firefighter.	
	do	your parents	**do**?	They**'re** scientists.	
Where	**does**	your sister	**work**?	She **works** in an animal hospital.	
		his uncle		He **works** in a firehouse.	
	do	your parents	**work**?	They **work** in a lab.	

Use *do* as the main verb to ask about a person's job: *What do your parents do?*

1 **Read and match.** Draw a line.

1. My father is a chef.
2. My uncle is a doctor.
3. My aunt is a nurse.
4. My grandfather is a vet.
5. My mother is a bus driver.

a. He works in a hospital.
b. She works on a bus.
c. He works in an animal hospital.
d. He works in a restaurant.
e. She works in a hospital.

2 **Read and write.**

1. What ________ your aunt do? ________ a firefighter.
2. What does your father ________? ________ a police officer.
3. What ________ your brother and sister ________? ________ farmers.
4. Where ________ your father work? He ________ at home.
5. Where does your sister ________? She ________ on a farm.

3 **Read.** Write questions.

1. ______________________? My brother is a singer.
2. ______________________? My mother is a teacher.
3. ______________________? My father works on a bus.
4. ______________________? My grandparents work in a school.

4 **Look and write.**

1. 

What does she do? ______________________.

Where does she work? ____________ a restaurant.

2. 

What does he do? ______________________.

Where does he work? ____________ an animal hospital.

3. 

What does she do? ______________________.

Where does she work? ____________ a hospital.

4. 

What do they do? ______________________.

Where do they work? ____________ the city.

5 **Write.** What do your parents do? Where do they work? Write about one or both parents.

____

____

Simple present with *want* + infinitive

Question					Answer
What	do	you	**want**	**to be**?	I **want to be** a police officer.
	does	your brother			He **wants to be** a scientist.
	do	your cousins			They **want to be** movie stars.

Use the verb *want* + *to be* to ask about a future job.

1 **Read and match.** Draw a line.

1. She likes to sing.
2. My brother plays soccer every day.
3. My sister likes to draw plants and flowers.
4. They can make new things very well.
5. He likes animals.
6. They like to study animals.

a. He wants to be a vet.
b. She wants to be an artist.
c. She wants to be a rock star.
d. They want to be scientists.
e. He wants to be a soccer player.
f. They want to be inventors.

2 **Read.** Circle the words.

1. What **do** / **does** you want to be?
   I **want** / **wants** to be an inventor.
2. What do your friends **want** / **wants** to be?
   They **want** / **wants** to be singers.
3. What **do** / **does** he want to be?
   He **want** / **wants** to be an artist.
4. What does your aunt **want** / **wants** to be?
   She wants **to be** / **being** a police officer.

3 Look and write.

1.  What do you want to be?

   ______________________________.

2.  What do your brother and sister want to be?

   ______________________________.

3.  What does your aunt want to be?

   ______________________________.

4 **Look.** Write questions and answers with *want to be*.

1.  you ______________________________?

   ______________________________.

2.  your brother ______________________________?

   ______________________________.

3.  your friend ______________________________?

   ______________________________.

5 **Write.** What do your friends want to be? Write 2 questions and answers.

What do you want to be, Scott?

I want to be a movie star.

____

____

____

____

Unit 2

Questions and answers with *any*

Question				Answer					
Is	there	**any**	meat?	Yes,	there	is.			*isn't = is not*
			pasta?	No,	there	isn't	**any**	pasta.	
Are	there	**any**	tomatoes?	Yes,	there	are.			*aren't = are not*
			beans?	No,	there	aren't	**any**	beans.	

There isn't any pasta = There is no pasta.

1 Read. Circle the words.

1. **Are** / **Is** there any potatoes? Yes, there **are** / **any**.
2. Is there **any** / **a** ice cream? No, there **isn't** / **aren't** any ice cream.
3. **Are** / **Is** there any corn? Yes, there **any** / **is**.
4. Are there any **mango** / **mangoes**? **Yes** / **No**, there are 3 mangoes.
5. Are there any **noodle** / **noodles**? No, there aren't **noodle** / **any noodles**.
6. Is there **any** / **a** water? No, there **isn't** / **aren't** any water.

2 Read and write.

1. Are there __any__ potatoes? No, there aren't __any__.
2. Is there ________ meat? Yes, there ________.
3. ________ there any beans? No, there ________ any.
4. ________________ tomatoes? Yes, ________________.
5. ________________ bread? No, ________________.
6. ________________ corn? Yes, ________________.

3 **Look.** Write questions and answers.

1. ice cream Is there any ice cream ?
No, there isn't any ice cream .
2. tomatoes ______________________________?
______________________________.
3. bread ______________________________?
______________________________.
4. meat ______________________________?
______________________________.
5. milk ______________________________?
______________________________.
6. mangoes ______________________________?
______________________________.

4 **Draw and write.** Draw a picture of your dinner. Write 2 questions and answers.

____
____
____
____

Polite requests with *may*

Question					Answer
May	**I**	have	some	yogurt?	Not now. Dinner is at 6:00.
					Yes. Sure.

Use *May I . . .* to make a polite request.

1 Read. Circle the word.

1. May I have **some** / **any** grapes?
2. **May** / **Is there** I have some yogurt, please?
3. **Yes** / **No**. Sure.
4. **Yes** / **No**. Not right now.
5. May we have some nuts, **thanks** / **please**?
6. May I have **some** / **any** meat?

2 Read and write. Find the mistake. Correct the question.

1. I have some may bread, please?
   May I have some bread, please ?
2. May we some ice cream have, please?
   ____?
3. We may some yogurt have, please?
   ____?
4. May I have grapes some, please?
   ____?
5. We may have some nuts, please?
   ____?

3 Look and write.

1. 

May I have some noodles, please?

☺ Yes, here you are.

2. 

3. 

4. 

5. 

6. 

4 **Draw and write.** You want to eat, but it's not time for dinner. Draw a comic. Ask your parents for something to eat. What do they say?

Unit 3

before and *after*

Question						Answer
What	does	she	do	**before**	school?	She feeds her fish.
	do	you		**after**	breakfast?	I get dressed.

Time phrases (with *before* and *after*) in a sentence show the order of two events.

1 **Look.** Write *before* or *after*.

Before dinner	After dinner

1. The children read ________________ dinner.
2. The boy combs his cat ________________ dinner.
3. The boy does his homework ________________ dinner.
4. He takes a shower ________________ dinner.
5. The baby and the boy play ________________ dinner.
6. The boy feeds his dog ________________ dinner.

2 **Write.** Unscramble the questions about Marta's day.

1. Marta / do / school / does / after / what

   What does Marta do after school ?

2. does / before / what / Marta / dinner / do

   ______________________________?

3. dinner / she / do / does / what / after

   ______________________________?

4. before / what / does / bedtime / do / she

   ______________________________?

3 **Read and write.** Look at Marta's schedule. Answer the questions from Activity 2. Use *before* and *after*.

4:00 school ends

4:30 take dog to the park

6:00 do homework

7:00 eat dinner

8:30 feed dog

8:45 brush teeth

9:00 bedtime

1. She takes her dog to the park after school.
2. ______________________________.
3. ______________________________.
4. ______________________________.

4 **Write.** What do you do? Use *before* or *after*.

1. ______________________________ dinner.
2. ______________________________ school.
3. ______________________________ dinner.
4. ______________________________ bedtime.

Adverbs of frequency

Omar	**always**	gets up	early.	
He	**usually**	eats	breakfast	at 6:00.
	sometimes			at 6:30.
He	**never**	makes	his bed.	

Use words like *always* and *sometimes* to describe how often you do an action.

1 **Read.** Write the word that is true for you.

always never sometimes usually

1. I ________________ eat breakfast before school.
2. I ________________ help with dinner.
3. I ________________ play soccer after school.
4. I ________________ get up at five o'clock in the morning.
5. I ________________ read before bed.
6. I ________________ play with my friends after school.
7. I ________________ make my bed in the morning.
8. I ________________ take a shower before I go to bed.

2 Look and write.

	M	T	W	T	F
Tamara / Ride bike	✓	✓	✓	✓	✓
Kiko / Take dog to park		✓	✓		
Olga / Do homework before school					
Marco / Help at home	✓	✓	✓		✓

Tamara ______________________________.

Kiko ______________________________.

Olga ______________________________.

Marco ______________________________.

3 **Read and write.** Answer the questions.

1. Who always makes breakfast at home?

______________________________.

2. Who sometimes helps you with your homework?

______________________________.

3. Who usually gets up before you?

______________________________.

4 **Write.** Tell what you do on weekends. Use *always, never, sometimes*, and *usually*.

I never get up before seven o'clock on Saturday.

____

____

Unit 4

Can for requests and offers

		Can	you	help	me?
Sure.	How	**can**	I	help?	

<table>
<tr><td rowspan="6">Where's the museum?</td><td rowspan="6">It's</td><td>on</td><td>Main Street.</td><td rowspan="6">where's = where is
it's = it is</td></tr>
<tr><td>next to</td><td>the police station.</td></tr>
<tr><td>across from</td><td>the bakery.</td></tr>
<tr><td>on the corner of</td><td>Main Street and First Street.</td></tr>
<tr><td>behind</td><td>the movie theater.</td></tr>
<tr><td>between</td><td>the park and the school.</td></tr>
</table>

Use *can* to ask for and to offer help.

1 Read and draw. Label your drawings.

1. The museum is across from the hospital.
2. The park is behind the house.
3. The bakery is next to the restaurant.

2 Write. Unscramble the questions. Add punctuation marks.

1. help / you / please / can / me

____

2. I / can / sure / how / help

____

3. supermarket / where / is / the

____

3 **Look at the map.** Complete the sentences.

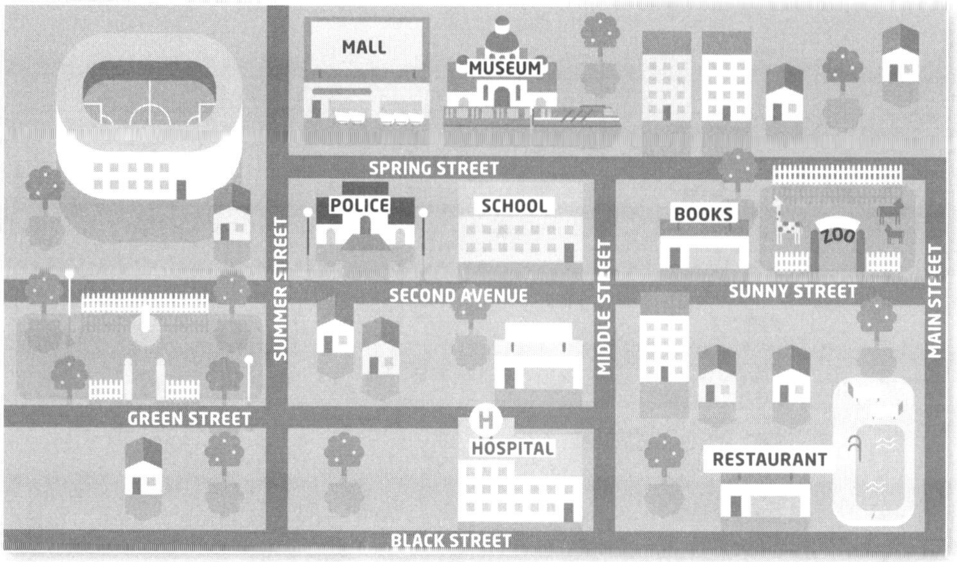

1. The school is ________________ Spring Street and Second Avenue.
2. The museum is ________________ the school.
3. The hospital is ________________ Middle Street and Black Street.
4. The school is ________________ the police station.

4 **Look and write.** Complete the dialogues. Use the map from Activity 3.

1. ________________ you ________________ me, please?

   ________________. ________________ can I help?

   ________________ the school?

   It's ________________________.

2. ________________ you ________________, please?

   Sure. ________________?

   ________________ the police station?

   It's on the corner of ________________________________.

Giving directions

Question	Answer			
How can I get to the post office?	**Go**	**straight**. (↑)		
	Turn	**right** (↱)	on	White Street.
		left (↰)	at	the supermarket.

Use the base form of verbs like *go* and *turn* to give directions.

1 Look and circle.

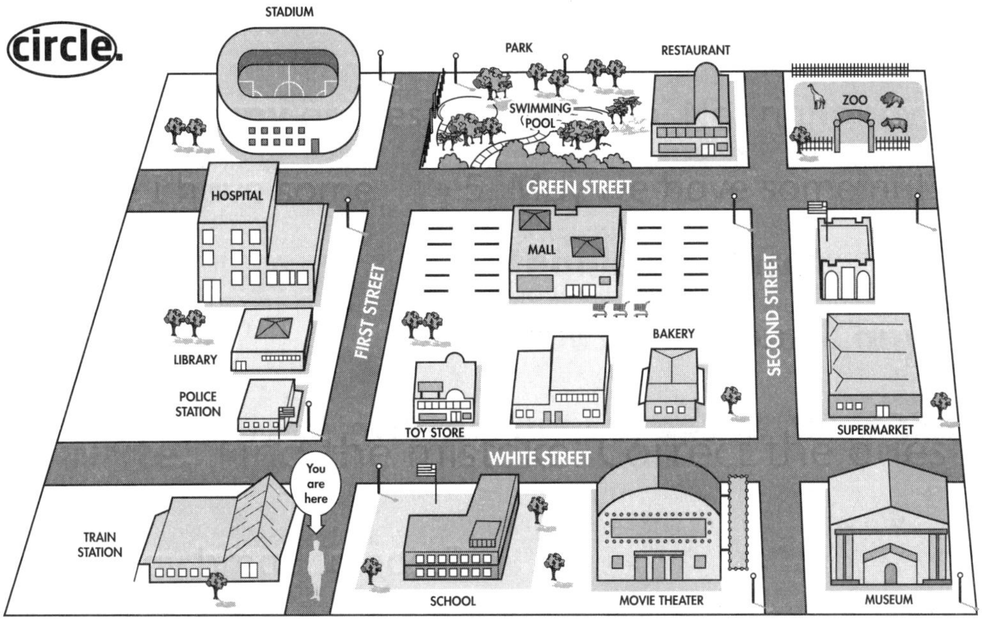

1. **How can I get to / Can you help me** the police station?

   Go straight on / Turn left on First Street.

   The police station is **across from / on the corner of** the toy store.

2. **How can I get to / Can you help me,** please?

   Yes, sure.

   How can I get to / How can I help the swimming pool?

   Turn **left / right** on Green Street. It's **between / across from** the park and the restaurant.

3. **How's / How can I get to** the stadium?

   Turn left on / Go straight on First Street.

   Turn left on Green Street. / Turn right on Second Street.

   It's across from the **post office / hospital.**

2 **Look and write.** Use the map in Activity 1.

1. How can ______________ the zoo?

   ______________ on First Street. ______________ on Green Street. It's ______________ the restaurant.

2. ______________ to the supermarket?

   ______________ on White Street. It's ______________ Second Street and White Street.

3. ______________ the hospital?

   ______________ on First Street. ______________ on Green Street. It's ______________ the stadium.

3 **Look again at the map in Activity 1.** Write directions.

1. How can I get to the restaurant?

   ____

   ____

2. How can I get to the mall?

   ____

   ____

4 **Write.** Give directions from your school to your house.

____

____

____

Unit 5

Too for agreeing

Statement				**Agreeing**			**Not agreeing**			
I	ride	my bike	to school.	I	**do**,	**too**.	I	**don't**.	I walk.	*don't = do not*
Eva	takes	the bus		Her friend	**does**,	**too**.	Her friend	**doesn't**.	She drives.	*doesn't = does not*

Use the pattern subject + *do/does* + *too* when you agree with a statement.

1 **Read and write.** Replace the underlined words.

1. I <u>do not</u> ride a scooter. — I ____________ ride a scooter.
2. My brother <u>does not</u> like airplanes. — He ____________ like airplanes.
3. My mom <u>does not</u> drive a car. — She ____________ drive a car.
4. My friends <u>do not</u> ride their bikes to school. — They ____________ ride their bikes to school.

2 **Write.** Give true information.

1. I want to take the ferry. — I do, too.
2. I go fast on my bike. —
3. I ride a scooter. —
4. My mom drives me to school. —
5. My dad walks a lot. —

3 **Look and write.** Complete the sentences.

Place	Scooter	Subway	Taxi	Bike
Museum		Paula	George/me	
Park	George			Paula/me
Grandparents' house	me	Paula/George		
Mall		me	George	Paula

1. I take a taxi to the museum.

George ___does, too___.
Paula ___doesn't___.
She ___takes the subway___.

2. Paula rides her bike to the park.

I ________________.
George ________________.
He ________________.

3. George takes the subway to his grandparents' house.

Paula ________________.
I ________________.
I ________________.

4. I take the subway to the mall.

Paula ________________.
She ________________.
George ________________.
He ________________.

4 **Write.** Think of a friend. Write three things you both do. Write two things you do differently.

I play soccer. José does, too. José plays baseball. I don't.

____

____

____

____

But as a contrast

My sister takes a taxi to the mall,	**but**	my brother rides his bike.

Use *but* to show contrast between two ideas in a sentence.

1 **Read.** Circle *and* or *but.*

1. Maya wants to go in a helicopter, **and** / **but** Dave does, too.
2. I don't take the subway very often, **and** / **but** my mom takes it every day.
3. I want to stay on the bus, **and** / **but** the driver says we must get off.
4. I go downhill fast, **and** / **but** Robert does, too.
5. My brother has a motorcycle, **and** / **but** I have a scooter.

2 **Read.** Write *but* when necessary. If *but* is not necessary, put an *X.*

1. We like reading, ______________ they like watching TV.
2. I have a red scooter, ______________ and Jon has one, too.
3. Giraffes have long necks ______________ and long legs.
4. I can walk to the zoo, ______________ Jaime can't. He takes the subway.
5. The train is fast, ______________ the bus is slow.

3 **Write.** Tell what's different.

1. A motorcycle is big, but a scooter is small. (a scooter)
2. My scooter has two wheels, ______________________________. (our car)
3. My dad takes the subway, ______________________________. (mom / bus)
4. Sandra rides her bike at the park, ______________________________. (walk my dog)
5. A boat goes on water, ______________________________. (a helicopter)

4 **Look and write.** Complete the sentences with *but*.

Me	My friend

1. I walk, ______________________________.

2. I play baseball, ______________________________.

3. I have a cat, ______________________________.

4. I eat yogurt, ______________________________.

5 **Write.** Write four sentences about friends and family. Use the words in the box and *but*.

be	eat	go	have	like	want	wear

I am young, but my grandfather is old.

____

____

Unit 6

Sense verbs

The pizza	**smells**	great.	The helicopter	**sounds**	loud.
The dress	**looks**	beautiful.	The cat	**feels**	soft.

Question				**Answer**		
How	does	the apple	**taste**?	It	**tastes**	delicious.
	do	the rabbits	**feel**?	They	**feel**	soft.

Words like *smell, look, sound,* and *feel* are not usually used in the progressive:
~~*The soup is tasting delicious.*~~

1 **Read and draw.** Draw an object for each sentence.

1. It tastes delicious.
2. It smells terrible.
3. It sounds loud.

2 **Read.** Answer the questions.

1. How does a motorcycle sound? It *sounds loud* ________________.
2. How does a rabbit feel? It ________________.
3. How does a banana taste? It ________________.
4. How does a bakery smell? It ________________.
5. How does a colorful dress look? It ________________.

3 Look and write.

1. 

How does the trash smell?

It smells terrible.

2. 

3. 

4. 

4 **Write.** Use words from each column.

airplanes		beautiful
coffee	feel	delicious
cookies	look	hard
my bed	sound	loud
paintings	taste	soft
a rock		terrible

1. A rock feels hard.
2. ______.
3. ______.
4. ______.
5. ______.
6. ______.

was/were

Question	Answer	Question			Answer			
How is the bread?	It's good.	How	**was**	the bread?	It	**was**	good.	*it's = it is*
How are the grapes?	They're good.	How	**were**	the grapes?	They	**were**	good.	*they're = they are*

There are two forms for the past tense of the verb *be*: *was* and *were*

1 **Read and match.** Draw a line.

1. How is your new bed?
2. How was the tomato soup?
3. How are your brothers?
4. How is the swimming pool?
5. How were the beans?

a. They were salty.
b. It was hot.
c. It's soft.
d. They're great!
e. It's big.

2 **Read and write.** Use the words in the box.

hard	sweet	terrible	well

1. How is your grandma? She ______________ very ______________, thank you.
2. How are the new chairs? They ______________ very ______________.
3. How were the cookies? They ______________ ______________.
4. How was the movie? It ______________ ______________!

3 **Write.** Use words from the box or your own.

delicious	easy	fun	terrible	well

1. How was your breakfast this morning? ______________________.
2. How is your best friend? ______________________.
3. How was your homework? ______________________.
4. How are your classes? ______________________.

4 **Look and write.** Use the correct tense.

~~bitter~~	salty	sour	spicy	sweet

1.  (before) How was the tea?
   It was bitter!
2.  (now) ______________________
   ____
3.  (before) ______________________
   ____
4.  (now) ______________________
   ____
5.  (before) ______________________
   ____

Unit 7

Why . . . ?/Because . . .

Question				**Answer**		
Why	do	snakes	come out during the day?	**Because**	they	like the sun.
	don't	you	like crocodiles?		they	are scary.
	can	frogs	jump high?		they	have strong legs.
	can't	birds	climb trees?		they	don't have arms.

Use *because* to answer a question with *why*.

1 Read and write.

1. ______________ does a hippo like mud? ______________ it wants to keep cool.
2. ______________ is a giraffe's neck so long? ______________ the giraffe eats leaves from tall trees.
3. ______________ can't penguins fly? ______________ their wings are better for swimming.
4. ______________ don't horses have stripes like zebras? ______________ they don't have to hide in the grass.

2 Read and write. Write *why* or *because* and words from the box.

bats	caves	scared

ANA: Let's explore this cave, Carlos.

CARLOS: No, thanks. I don't like caves.

ANA: ______________ don't you like ______________?

CARLOS: ______________ ______________ live in caves.

ANA: ______________ don't you like bats?

CARLOS: ______________ I'm ______________ of them.

3 Write questions.

1. a giraffe / be tall Why is a giraffe tall ______?
2. elephants / can't fly ______?
3. a bird / make a nest ______?
4. kangaroos / have pouch ______?

4 **Write.** Answer the questions from Activity 3.

1. Because it eats leaves from tall trees ______.
2. ______.
3. ______.
4. ______.

5 **Write.** Think of a famous person to interview, such as a singer. Write four questions with *why*. Then write the answers.

Why do you sing in English? Because I'm from Canada.

Infinitive of purpose

Parrots	use	their	wings	**to fly**.	
Cats			tongues	**to clean**	their fur.
Kangaroos			pouches	**to carry**	their babies.

To + verb describes how or why we do something to reach a goal.

1 Read. Circle *to* or *because*.

1. Why do frogs use their back legs?

   Frogs use their back legs **because** / **to** jump.

2. Why does an owl have big eyes?

   Because / **To** it needs to see at night.

3. Why do tigers have sharp teeth?

   Because / **To** they need them to eat meat.

4. Why do penguins have wings?

   Penguins have wings **because** / **to** swim in the sea.

5. Why do kangaroos have pouches?

   Kangaroos have pouches **because** / **to** carry their babies inside.

2 Read and write. Use words from the box.

catch ~~clean~~ drink fly run stay

1. Giraffes use their tongues ___to clean___ their ears.
2. Bears use their fur ________________ warm.
3. Lions use their sharp claws ________________ other animals.
4. Elephants use their trunks ________________ water.
5. Ostriches use their long legs ________________ fast.
6. Parrots use their wings ________________.

3 Read and write. Use *to.*

1. What do you use to carry your books?

   I use a backpack to carry my books__________.

2. What do you use to brush your teeth?

   ____________________.

3. What do you use to talk to friends?

   ____________________.

4. Why do you study and do your homework?

   ____________________.

4 Write. Write sentences with *to.*

1. frogs / long tongue

   Frogs use their long tongues to catch flies__________.

2. butterflies / wings

   ____________________.

3. monkeys / hands

   ____________________.

4. owls / big eyes

   ____________________.

5 Write. Write four sentences about your body.

I use my nose to smell flowers.__________

____

____

____

Unit 8

some* and *any

Question				Answer					
Are	there	**any**	eggs?	Yes,	there	are	**some**	on the table.	*aren't = are not*
			apples?	No,	there	aren't	(**any**).		
Is	there	**any**	cheese?	Yes,	there	is	**some**	in the fridge.	*isn't = is not*
			rice?	No,	there	isn't	(**any**).		

Use *some* and *any* to talk about general amounts.

1 **Look and match.** Draw a line.

1. Is there any cheese?
2. Are there any olives?
3. Are there any cookies?
4. Is there any sugar?

a. Yes, there are some.
b. Yes, there is some.
c. No, there isn't any.
d. No, there aren't any.

2 **Read.** Write *some* or *any*.

1. Is there ____any____ orange juice? Yes, there is ____some____.
2. Is there ________ cake? No, there isn't ________.
3. Are there ________ cans of soda? Yes, there are ________.
4. Is there ________ milk? No, there isn't ________.
5. Are there ________ bananas? Yes, there are ________.
6. Are there ________ tomatoes? No, there aren't ________.

3 **Write.** Complete the questions and answers.

1. Are there any banana s? → 1. __Are there any__ bananas?

   Yes, __there are some__.

2. ______________ slices of bread?

   No, ______________.

3. ______________ oil for cooking?

   Yes, ______________.

4. strawberry yogurt in the refrigerator?

   No, ______________.

4 **Look and write questions.** Look in your kitchen for answers.

1. 

   Are there any olives?

   No, there aren't any olives in my kitchen.

2. 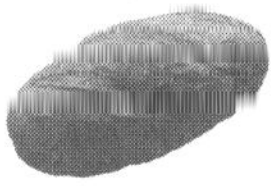

   ____

   ____

3. 

   ____

   ____

4. 

   ____

5. 

   ____

   ____

a few and *a little*

Question				Answer					
Are	there	any	nuts?	Yes,	there	are	**a few**	on the table.	*aren't = are not*
			olives?	No,	there	aren't	(any).		
Is	there	any	juice?	Yes,	there	is	**a little**	in the bottle.	*isn't = is not*
			tea?	No,	there	isn't	(any).		

Use *a few* and *a little* to talk about general amounts.

1 **Read.** Cross out foods that don't belong.

A few	A little
tomatoes	milk
~~tea~~	~~sandwiches~~
oil	grapes
soup	sugar
nuts	cans of soda
cereal	bread
noodles	pizza

2 **Read.** Circle the correct answer.

1. Are there any olives? Yes, there are **a little** / **a few**.
2. Is there any cereal? Yes, there's **a little** / **a few** in the box.
3. Is there any juice? Yes, there is **a little** / **a few** in the fridge.
4. Are there any cookies? Yes, there are **a little** / **a few**.
5. Is there any sugar? Yes, there's **a little** / **a few** in the sugar bowl.
6. Are there any potatoes? Yes, there are **a little** / **a few** in the bag.

3 **Look at the picnic.** Complete the conversations.

1. Are there any olives?
   Yes, there are a few.
2. ______ cake?
   ______
3. ______ bananas?
   ______
4. ______ ice cream?
   ______
5. ______ milk?
   ______
6. ______ grapes?
   ______

4 **Read.** Complete the sentences.

In my refrigerator, there ______ milk, and there ______ orange juice. There ______ eggs on the top shelf, and there ______ butter, too. There ______ yogurt, and there ______ red strawberries in a bowl. On the bottom shelf, there ______ tomatoes, and there ______ grapes. What's in your refrigerator?

5 **Write.** Tell what's in your refrigerator.

______

______